CODE
BILLY II

75 Real Life Meditations

JIM MARSHALL

🐦 dustjacket

DEDICATION

It is my honor and privilege to dedicate this second volume of CODE BILLY to my dear friends Rev. Lee and Beverley DeSaulnier.

Most of us can count on one hand the people who have had a major impact on our lives, not counting parents. Lee and Bev fit this category for me.

When Marg and I were first married we moved to Portland, Oregon, to go to seminary and to work for World Gospel Mission in their Western Office. Lee was the director and I became his assistant.

Lee taught me the discipline of punctuality, the importance of follow through and the vital need for consistency. His mentorship has served me well for over forty years in ministry.

Lee and "Bevo" showed my new bride and me how to be "fun Christians." They knew how to work and play hard. We accompanied them on a vacation to Knoxberry Farm and Disneyland, one that will never be forgotten. They became more than just associates; they are like family to us.

Lee just recently got to spend his first Christmas in heaven. Bev continues to serve God and her family in the beautiful state of Oregon.

I do not believe I would be writing these meditations without the godly influence of these two wonderful friends.

Thank You, Lord, for bringing them into our lives!

Jim and Marg Marshall

TABLE OF CONTENTS

KEY TO SCRIPTURE VERSES

KJV	King James Version
MSG	The Message
NLT	New Living Translation
LB	Living Bible
NKJV	New King James Version
MEV	Modern English Version
AMP	Amplified
NLV	New Life Version
GNT	Good News Translation
NIV	New International Version

PROLOGUE

"CODE BILLY"

After two weeks in ICU, two more weeks in the stroke ward, and seven weeks in rehab hospital, my daughter was released to go home. As last minute paperwork was being signed, an announcement came over the intercom saying, "Attention 2nd floor staff—Code Billy."

(A "Code Billy" — named after a patient who had spent many months in the hospital — was used to inform the staff that someone was getting to go home.)

One of the support people, who had assisted my daughter through her recovery days, now guided her wheelchair down the hall and onto the elevator with my wife, son and me in tow. As we rounded the corner on the 1st floor, ahead of us stood doctors, nurses and technicians lining the hallway applauding as we walked and rolled between them. Several were crying as our procession passed. It was a day of triumph for a patient who surpassed all their expectations. Mom and Dad joined in their tears of joy.

We go through life not knowing the future. Day by day we push ahead with our duties and schedules, trying to enjoy life to the fullest. When tragedy strikes and setbacks come, it makes us ask "Why?" We don't understand and can feel all alone.

But every once in a while, the curtain is pulled back and we get a glimpse of the love and support we do have. Family, friends, even strangers are lined up praying and pulling for us. It's a new day—we will walk again!

Hebrews 12: 1 *(New International Version)* Therefore, since we are surrounded by such a huge crowd of witnesses to the life of faith, let us strip off every weight that slows us down, especially the sin that so easily trips us up. And let us run with endurance the race God has set before us.

INCHING TOWARD THE COUNTER

I have a friend who gets to do extraordinary things because he obeys God's promptings without hesitation.

One of Dr. Baird's several earned doctorates is in dentistry. One day he was working on a patient when he sensed God telling him to get on the next flight to India. He immediately left his patient and told his administrative assistant to call in another doctor and to notify his wife, who by now, was quite used to her husband's schedule changes.

My friend went straight to the airport and was standing in line to buy a ticket. (before e-tickets) The only problem was he had no money or plastic to pay for the flight since he regularly gave away most of his funds for various ministries.

Inching ever closer to the counter he began to feel more and more silly. Was it really God who asked him to do this? It did not make sense. Finally, there was only one person ahead of him. At that moment a middle-aged couple stepped up and asked if he was Dr. Baird. He replied in his southern gentleman accent that he was.

After explaining that they hoped he didn't think it odd, they said, "We were waiting on our connecting flight and saw you in line. We felt God tell us to buy you a round trip ticket to India--would that be okay with you?"

The dentist said, "If you insist."

You may be facing a situation that has you inching toward a decision or a commitment and you have no idea how it can happen. For sure God does not ask all of us to take such risks as my friend; just know His provision can come in so many ways and often comes later rather than sooner.

As you inch toward your counter don't be afraid. The shorter the distance the greater our trust in Him must be. Maybe God will urge you to meet the need of someone else in line. Either way, God knows where you are, you can bank on it!

Philippians 4:19 KJV *But my God shall supply all your need according to His riches in glory by Christ Jesus.*

LEANING OVER THE COUNTER: THE REST OF THE STORY

With God's miraculous provision at the ticket counter, my dentist friend flew to India and landed in Calcutta. As he walked the streets he asked God what he was supposed to do in this incredibly poor city with hundreds of people dying in the alleyways each day.

As the doctor progressed through the city, he noticed a disheveled little man leaning up against a building and felt drawn to him. As he approached the man afflicted with leprosy (an Untouchable in that society), my medical friend literally had to move away several times and vomit because of the sickening smell. Finally, he was able to sit down on the ground next to the crumpled-up man, put his arm around the man's shoulder, and asked if he knew Jesus as his personal savior. A smile came across the creased lips of this leper in reply to the question and then he died in the doctor's arms.

As this learned, compassionate physician sat on the ground thousands of miles from his hometown of Louisville, Kentucky, he simply asked God why he was brought all the way to India to watch a man die. The answer came: "I brought you here just to show you that I love this man as much as I love you. You can return home now."

We all have to make final preparations for our final flight. Only a personal relationship with Jesus Christ can purchase this one-way ticket. The Ticketmaster is leaning over the heavenly counter to provide us safe passage. Take it!

Psalm 18:6   LB   *In my distress I screamed to the Lord for His help. And He heard me from heaven; my cry reached His ears.*

A TIME FOR MIRACLES

Christmas is many things to many people. If you sub-scribe to the biblical account of the Christmas story you must deduce it was all quite miraculous. From the virgin birth to the guiding star to the subsequent hiatus in Egypt, the Savior's birth ushered in a series of unexplainable phenomena that must be received by faith to be fully appreciated.

Interestingly, humans have not changed all that much over 2000 years. We still have our job routines like the shepherds. Many continue to study the stars for guidance like the Wise-men. Taxation, poverty and the search for a better life continue to dominate our world. The twelfth month brings on many added stresses as we overload our schedules and stretch our resources to "celebrate" the holiday season.

Let us not overlook that, at its essence, Christmas is a time for miracles. If you're needy in any way you're a candidate for a miracle. Truth is, many miracles happen all around us but we tend to not see them because we're moving too fast or are distracted by our busyness.

Slow down, look up and stay tuned. God knows what you need, His timing is flawless.

Luke 2:8-11 LB *That night some shepherds were in the fields outside the village, guarding their flocks of sheep. Suddenly an angel appeared among them, and the landscape shone bright with the glory of the Lord. They were badly frightened, but the angel reassured them. "Don't be afraid!" he said. "I bring you the most joyful news ever announced, and it is for everyone! The Savior—yes, the Messiah, the Lord—has been born tonight in Bethlehem!*

ALL SHE HAD TO SAY WAS...

I tried to pick up some of my clothes from the cleaners. After an extensive search it was discovered that my shirt was missing and no one knew where it might be. I was asked to come back in a few days to see if it had been returned.

I purposely was kind and extra patient because I knew the woman was embarrassed. It was simply disappointing to not get my shirt when I needed it.

These things happen so we have to deal with them. Had she said she was sorry, that would have helped a whole bunch.

All of us encounter these types of situations from time to time; in fact, it almost seems to be more the norm these days. The reasons for the "indifferent attitude" are varied. Some say it's the breakdown of the home--people are not taught manners anymore. Others indicate that our automated, computerized world has contributed to diminished people skills. Whatever the cause, rude behavior is unacceptable and a great challenge to employers as they conduct business. The ads promote warm, caring service but reality often displays the opposite.

Truth is, each of us works and serves customers in some area of our life. Things go wrong; we have a bad day; someone messes up and we have to fix it. Sincerely apologizing goes a long way in helping to calm the atmosphere, to focus on the one who was wronged rather than scramble for our alibi. No, it does not find "our shirt," but it does unite us to continue the search.

Our relationship with God is also maintained when we admit we are wrong and seek forgiveness.

Matthew 7:12 MSG *Here is a simple, rule-of-thumb guide for behavior: Ask yourself what you want people to do for you, then grab the initiative and do it for them. Add up God's Law and the Prophets and this is what you get.*

DESTINATION: EXCELLENCE

One day I pulled up next to an eighteen wheeler that had these words written on the cab: "Destination: Excellence." This caught my attention and made me think of some implications.

We are all on a journey headed somewhere. Striving for excellence makes the trip much more rewarding for us as well as others. In the case of flying, I've been fortunate to go first class several times. Because of the quality of the flight, my destination was automatically enhanced.

The daily quest for excellence is a great antidote for "destination disease." It's easy to wish we were already there, especially when the daily grind seems to be getting to us.

Most of us have lived long enough to understand that the pursuit is usually better than the achievement. We dream of accomplishment, of acquiring something and then, when we have it, often it does not live up to its advance billing.

Our all-powerful God, who created this world with all its beauty and mystery in a week, has been away from earth almost 2000 years preparing a place for us. Imagine how magnificent and excellent heaven must be after all this time!

No matter what, make sure heaven is your final destination.

Philippians 4:8-9 MSG *Summing it all up, friends, I'd say you'll do best by filling your minds and meditating on things true, noble, reputable, authentic, compelling, gracious—the best, not the worst; the beautiful, not the ugly; things to praise, not things to curse. Put into practice what you learned from me, what you heard and saw and realized. Do that, and God, who makes everything work together, will work you into His most excellent harmonies.*

AUTO PRAYING

Praying is something we all need to do, but it can be a struggle at times, especially with our packed schedules. So with the many needs and people to pray for, how can I remember to speak their name to God?

A method I use to pray is when I see a vehicle which looks like the car or truck of someone I know, I immediately say a prayer of blessing for that person and family, with my eyes open of course.

One day, while driving to my office, I recognized a van but couldn't remember the name of the person who owned it or one like it. Later in the day as I was reviewing my contact list the person's name appeared, and I was able to reinforce my earlier prayer. God's prompting to pray now made sense.

Our all-knowing God is not limited by our forgetfulness. He understands our motive and compensates for our deficiencies. Our part is to pray.

I'm hoping you will "auto pray" for me. I need it. We all do!

2 Timothy 1:3a   MSG   *Every time I say your name in prayer—which is practically all the time—I thank God for you...*

CUSTOMER IN TRAINING

I was in a grocery store one day and observed a mother shopping with her young daughter. The little girl was pushing a miniature shopping cart with a pole and flag attached which said "Customer in Training."

In addition to being an excellent incentive for family shopping, it also reflected a much larger issue: namely, that each of us is in training, a work in process. We don't really see ourselves this way for we are continually being pushed from every direction to "grow up," "be mature," "take responsibility," and even "self-actualize." Reality checks in and says life is not quite that formulated.

Striving for excellence and improvement must never cease. At the same time, we must cut ourselves a little slack, to acknowledge our humanity--that we are in training and have not yet arrived.

Our Lord's actions toward people indicate His patience. Scripture seems to reveal His displeasure with those who pretended to have it all together while being hypercritical of others who were struggling.

Excuses are not allowed, but tolerance always is. Be good to yourself today. Understand you are in training. Your disposition will enable you to assist others as they "push their carts."

James 1:2-4 MSG *Consider it a sheer gift, friends, when tests and challenges come at you from all sides. You know that under pressure, your faith-life is forced into the open and shows its true colors. So don't try to get out of anything prematurely. Let it do its work so you become mature and well-developed, not deficient in any way.*

BE DANGEROUS

Phrases like "staying in your comfort zone" or "working within your limits" can actually be good advice. A new friend spoke to me as he was walking away… "Be dangerous." It set me back for I've never been admonished like that. Usually people say things like "Take it easy," or "Be careful," or "Have a safe trip." But, to be dangerous, what's up with that?

After thinking about what my friend stated, I realize this is godly advice. Taking risks, living on the edge, needs to be more of the norm for a Christian. Any honest reading of scripture illustrates that many of those God used were "dangerous" like Samson and Paul. In other words, they obeyed God no matter how ridiculous his commands seemed to them.

Heroes of the faith like Noah and Moses were not superstars or celebrities, but ordinary people whom God could trust to impact their world. Christ set the example; He did not play it safe. The entire plan of salvation was very risky;

there certainly was no guarantee humans would accept God's son.

Yet, Jesus came anyway to a dangerous world and showed us how to live: Not somehow but Triumphantly.

Numbers 13:30 LB *But Caleb reassured the people as they stood before Moses. "Let us go up at once and possess it," he said, "for we are well able to conquer it!"*

FIRST THINGS LAST

While serving as a missionary/pastor in Kenya, Africa, I learned many valuable lessons. One that stands out is that when visiting someone, you always save your real reason for the visit until you are about to leave. Up till that time you talk about everything else like the weather, children, pets--you name it. It is a pleasant way to get to know each other, to accept hospitality and to relax. In our "western world" we have replaced this neighborly custom with the "bottom line" and "cut to the chase" mentality. It has not improved our society.

We would do well to learn from our African friends--to slow down and enjoy each other's company rather than promoting our own agenda. In our "smart phone" world it's so easy to trade high tech for high touch, resulting in shallow relationships. Everyone loses with this model and we must correct it.

Where do we start? I suggest we begin with our Maker. Since we are made in His image, He is very much like us. Imagine how He must feel when we rush in with our orders and then depart without as much as a "thank you" or any sort of meaningful sharing? No relationship can endure very long on the surface.

Revising our "settings" so that friendship and worship respectively precede business and requests will greatly elevate our standard of living, no matter where we reside.

Psalm 46:10a KJV *Be still, and know that I am God.*

BECOMING A CANDY PERSON

I attended an inspiring funeral service where I learned that the deceased gentleman was known in the community as the "Candy Man." He gave out candy to everyone he met, especially to kids. This generous act, along with other winsome traits, endeared him to hundreds of people.

All of us are giving out something to other people whether we know it or not. Oh, it may not be tangible, but our attitudes and physical demeanor continually send out signals which either encourage or discourage others. The latter has no place in the life of one who wants to be like Christ.

In order to become a "Candy Person" (someone who sweetens any situation) we will have to be proactive. Here are a few suggestions:

1. Find a sweet person and hang out with them. Becoming a "Candy Person" is more caught than taught. It will require watching and copying your model.

2. Ingest sweet things into your mind. Thinking tastefully precedes acting tastefully. Positive input is necessary if our output is to help anyone. Scripture can really assist us in this effort.

3. Realize this is a process and not an event. Unlike the "Candy Man" most of us do not come by this naturally. We need lots of practice and must be patient with ourselves.

4. Don't feel you have to accomplish this by yourself. Make sure someone who loves you helps you in this transformation by giving you progress reports.

Being a "Candy Person" is not just a nice thing to do; it literally sweetens your life.

Proverbs 16:24   NLT   *Kind words are like honey—sweet to the soul and healthy for the body.*

CHARACTER DOES COUNT

How does a Christian respond to the behavior of our nation's leaders and potential leaders?

Consider the following ideas as you strive to be an authentic believer:

Above All, Pray for Your Leaders. Scripture commands it of us. We can do nothing better than pray, especially when so much is at stake.

Keep Your Brain in Gear. Of all people, Christians ought to be thinking clearly. Even though "common sense" is not all that common today, don't abandon yours. God's spirit will help you discern truth from error if you stay in touch with Him.

Stay in the Word. God's "game plan" tells us how to live in all kinds of weather. It gives us perspective and reaffirms that right living ultimately wins.

Don't Confuse Charisma with Character. We live in a poll-driven society where the end often justifies the means. It seems if one can perform and please the public then it doesn't matter what kind of personal life that person may lead. This is as good as humanism gets.

We are Judged by Our Heart, not Our Personality. The Bible indicates that we look on the outward appearance but God sees right through us. Therefore, our public and private lives must be consistent. D.L. Moody wrote, "The only way to tell if a stick is crooked is to place it alongside a straight one."

1 Timothy 4:12 NLT *Don't let anyone think less of you because you are young. Be an example to all believers in what you say, in the way you live, in your love, your faith, and your purity.*

IT NEVER ENTERED MY MIND
TO CHANGE MY MIND

It was my privilege to visit with a retired couple in my church who were celebrating 55 years of marriage. As we laughed and teased about staying together so long the wife made this statement: "It never entered my mind to change my mind." In other words, we got married for keeps, and it's still working.

In our fast-lane world we are challenged to change the way we do things in almost every area of life. Much of the change is ultimately for the better although it's hard to accept at first. However, some things should never be negotiable like our marriage and our relationship with God.

Many people allow negative thoughts to not only enter their minds but then welcome them to stay. These thoughts are destructive to our society and counter to our promise to stay with our mate till "death us do part." Strong, long-term relationships are no accident; you have to decide on the front end not to entertain thoughts of leaving your soul mate for any reason or anybody.

The same goes in our relationship with God. Whether you "feel" like it or not, decide to be in it for the long haul. These two relationships do more to elevate our society and enhance our life than anything else.

Ephesians 5:25-28 MSG *Husbands, go all out in your love for your wives, exactly as Christ did for the church—a love marked by giving, not getting. Christ's love makes the church whole. His words evoke her beauty. Everything He does and says is designed to bring the best out of her, dressing her in dazzling white silk, radiant with holiness. And that is how husbands ought to love their wives. They're really doing themselves a favor—since they're already "one" in marriage.*

CHIPPIN' AND CHOPPIN'

An acquaintance of mine, when asked how he is doing, invariably responds "I'm chippin' and choppin'." When I first heard his answer it sounded trite, but the more I think about it, this does describe much of life. We do "chip" and "chop" every day as we deal with people, projects and problems.

Now, it is true that people and projects and problems often overlap. But for clarification purposes, let's look at each category.

People. This category is the most difficult since the variables are nearly endless. Getting along with people, having them trust and respect you, (let alone like you,) is a lifelong job. It's never a done deal and so it involves a lot of chippin'. There are times when a rift in our relationship with someone requires us to boldly move and chop down the misunderstanding or offence. At those times we dare not comfortably chip away when a much more aggressive approach is needed.

Projects. Someone has said that we tend to overestimate what we can do in one year and underestimate what we can accomplish in five years. In other words, even though we like to chop so as to make visible progress, it's usually in the chippin' where true advances are made. Time, persistence and patience must be utilized as we try to get stuff done.

Problems. We know problems are a continual part of life. They are acceptable as long as we stay on top of them rather than vice-versa. Not all problems are the same so they demand different treatment. Some are chronic due to a weakness of character or a physical malady. Patiently chippin' away at these is the best we can do at times. Other challenges necessitate immediate action, to chop the issue out of our life. You dare not be comfortable just to chip at bitterness or cope with sin. These demand surgical removal from your spirit and, if not treated properly, will hurt others and destroy you.

Keep on chippin' and choppin'. You're probably accomplishing more than you know.

Romans 5:4   LB   *And patience develops strength of character in us and helps us trust God more each time we use it until finally our hope and faith are strong and steady.*

CLIMBING ON BUMPS

One day a little boy was leading his sister up a mountain path. The girl, disgusted by the difficulty of the hike, complained to her brother, "Why, it's not a path at all! It's all rocky and bumpy."

The boy replied, "Sure, the bumps are what you climb on."

Bumps are a fact of life, especially when we're moving in an upward direction. We can choose to stumble or step on them. Our choice is made at the outset; we do not evaluate each bump or obstacle and then decide what to do. Our predisposition towards our challenges ultimately determines whether we advance or retreat.

Climbing life's mountains goes so much better when we have a guide to help us. God never intended for us to make it alone. He wants to help but we have to trust Him enough so that whatever path He chooses we simply follow.

The unexplained blessings in our lives are His hands reaching out to us when we stumble.

Proverbs 3:5-6   NLT   *Trust in the LORD with all your heart; do not depend on your own understanding. Seek His will in all you do, and He will show you which path to take.*

COLLATERAL MIRACLES

Today's technology allows us to watch from the safety of our homes as drones launch precision weapons to destroy buildings which house our enemies. Their pinpoint accuracy is supposed to take out the target without bothering anyone else. In reality, non-combatants are accidentally killed and unintended damage is inflicted. All of this is referred to as the price of war or "collateral damage."

A more positive principle applies when it comes to miracles. We pray for someone by name and wait to see the answer. But, the One to whom we pray always has the higher ground and sees the big picture. He often helps, heals, saves, enlightens, provides and touches targets we do not expect. While the issue we pray for may still be active, other remedies are speeding their way to resolve surrounding problems and needs.

These collateral miracles come from the greatest bombardier of all time. He's never missed yet and that's good news!

Philippians 1:2 **LB** *May God bless you all. Yes, I pray that God our Father and the Lord Jesus Christ will give each of you His fullest blessings and His peace in your hearts and your lives.*

THE BEST CHRISMTAS PRESENT EVER

Have you ever been asked, "What's the best Christmas present you've ever received?" It makes you think and reminisce for most of us have been greatly blessed.

There is one gift we all need and that is PEACE. In our busy and complex world we seek a reprieve, a time out for rest and calm. Life can heat us up; Christmas time with all its extra demands and tensions can leave us totally depleted and not receptive to the meaning of Christ's birth. We go through the motions and have fleeting moments of joy only to be interrupted by the reality of things like finances, estranged relationships, medical difficulties and fear of the future.

The Prince of Peace came to give us not only eternal life but peace here and now. This gift differs from other gifts we receive. We must ask for it. Our Lord will not force peace upon us but has it available if we ask. In our asking we must first let go of all the "peace thieves" in our lives. This is not easy as many of us can attest; however, it's very possible and definitely God's will.

This peace is not the absence of problems or frustrations. It is knowing, in our hearts, that no matter what we're experiencing, He's in control just like He was that first Christmas. So, we can laugh and relax and enjoy.

Philippians 4:6-7 MSG *Don't fret or worry. Instead of worrying, pray. Let petitions and praises shape your worries into prayers, letting God know your concerns. Before you know it, a sense of God's wholeness, everything coming together for good, will come and settle you down. It's wonderful what happens when Christ displaces worry at the center of your life.*

HANG ON

Part of our initiation into life in Calgary, Alberta, Canada, was the 10-day rodeo show called the Stampede. Our church gave us white cowboy hats. My boots, bought earlier in Texas but hardly worn, now seemed "at home."

Rodeo events are much more difficult and exciting than one would think at first glance. They're all fun to watch but I especially enjoy the bull and bronc riding. The rider only has to stay on the animal for a few seconds which may seem like a "lifetime" since the steer or horse does its best to eject the cargo. Riders are only allowed to hold on with one hand while they balance themselves with the other as they bounce with each mighty buck.

Life, at times, is not too different from rodeo riding. The trials and challenges we experience can really send us flying. We often seem to be coming down while life is rising up which can result in a painful, jarring rendezvous. Before we can recover, the action is repeated and we wonder how much more can we take?

Just like the riders, all we have to do is hang on a little longer. Whatever we're going through will pass and relief will come. Hang on to your faith in yourself and in Almighty God. He's in the arena with you and so are others. Hang on to the fact that others love you and only want the best for you. Hang on to the good things you've been taught about God; He never works against you but continues to give freedom so you can serve Him willfully.

Hang on Friend! Payday is just ahead!

1 Corinthians 9:26-27   Phillips   *I run the race then with determination. I am no shadow-boxer, I really fight! I am my body's sternest master, for fear that when I have preached to others I should myself be disqualified.*

DON'T STRAY TOO FAR

Many of us can remember a parent or guardian instructing us to stay close to home because we'll be eating soon or company is coming. As children, we heard their admonition but sometimes would forget, especially as more "exciting" opportunities came along.

Adults are not much different. Yes, we certainly have more responsibility, but grownups too can stray from their moorings in the pursuit of adventure and fun. For the most part this is natural but can also have negative consequences, for in the time that we wander off from God, from the church and even from the morals we've been taught, there is great potential for disaster. The experiences we have do not compensate for the time wasted.

One place from which we dare not stray too far is Calvary, for it is there that our Death Penalty was paid. Our mission, should we choose to accept it, is to receive our pardon and stay close to the One who occupied the center cross.

It's almost suppertime.

Hebrews 3:15   LB *But now is the time. Never forget the warning, "Today if you hear God's voice speaking to you, do not harden your hearts against Him, as the people of Israel did when they rebelled against Him in the desert."*

PICKING THE WINNER

Football season is a great time for most sports fans. Teams of varying talent and resources hit the field wanting to win every game. Families and friends show up hoping their team will be victorious one more time. Many bet on the games--millions of dollars will pass to those who correctly "pick the winner." In spite of all the analysis used and strategies employed to make one team win and the other lose, no one knows for sure what the final outcome will be. The bounce of the ball still impacts the game.

The game of life has many similarities to football. For one, we must possess the ball in order to score, even with a safety. Also, without proper equipment we'll soon be injured and have to leave the game. Teamwork is the key to winning--no one player can do it alone. Often our forward progress is penalized by some infraction which could have been inadvertent. It's okay to be on the sidelines for a while. All of these concepts apply to both football and life.

One major difference in the game of life is we get to choose whose side we're on: Satan's or God's. This choice is no small thing for it literally determines where we'll be when we retire from this world. Our selection is very personal and, unlike betting, it does not take advantage of someone else's loss to make us win. God's team is already a winner--has been since our Captain, Jesus, defeated the evil team on Mount Calvary.

Good news! Life's game is highly interactive. We don't just spectate hoping our team will "pull it out." We are winners both now and later by being on the right team. Go God!

Exodus 32:26   MSG   *Moses saw that the people were simply running wild—Aaron had let them run wild, disgracing themselves before their enemies. He took up a position at the entrance to the camp and said, "Whoever is on God's side, join me!"*

DOWN BUT NOT OUT

Life certainly has its "down times" when we're unable to communicate the way we'd like or to stay in touch with others. We can feel distant, cut off and "out of it" if resolution delays. Discouragement can overwhelm us and we may think we've been left behind.

Truth is, "down times" can be therapeutic if we allow them to be. The pressure to answer every phone call, reply to every e-mail or text message, and stay in touch with family and friends can literally drain us. God would have us to pull back and regain our equilibrium by reading His words and reflecting on what's really important.

It has been said that it's okay to fall down nine times as long as we get up ten. Our challenge is to make our "off line" periods a time of refreshing, knowing that we're not out of it but just taking a break.

1 Peter 1:21   LB   ... *your trust can be in God who raised Christ from the dead and gave Him great glory. Now your faith and hope can rest in Him alone.*

GROWING OLDER

Celebrating birthdays is a big deal in our family. We try to make it "birthday week", even "month" if we can. I have been greatly blessed with a wonderful wife, four resourceful children and many close friends. Here are some things I have learned or am in the process of learning as each of my birthdays pass:

Getting Older is Inevitable: Our biological clock keeps on ticking and our body constantly changes. However, "growing" older is a choice which reminds me "I am a lifelong student." I choose to grow intellectually, emotionally and spiritually. These three areas require continual monitoring; they do not happen automatically. Cultivation of my mind and soul is vital if I'm to mature.

Liking the Real You: I have been living with me for many years. To grow I must accept myself. This does not mean you stop trying to improve but deliberately focus on your strengths rather than your weaknesses. For years you have tried to earn respect and be accepted. Bottom line is others will like you more when you genuinely like yourself.

Staying Ready to Go: To say that life is uncertain is a big understatement. Our world is more fragile than ever--we do not know what a day will bring. Therefore, it is imperative that we be ready to meet our Maker. True, significance is a legitimate goal but being right with God is our highest calling. To live forever with the "redeemed" equals ultimate success.

Titus 2:2-3a MEV *Older men should be sober, serious, temperate, sound in faith, in love, in patience. Likewise, older women should be reverent in behavior.*

ENJOY YOUR DAY

I was leaving a 7-Eleven store (many Canadian post offices are inside convenience stores and drug stores) when the clerk said, "Enjoy your day." His admonition caught me by surprise: no one had ever suggested this to me in quite this way before, especially not a stranger. It caused me to think.

Enjoyment is a choice. Of course we all want to have a "nice day", one wherein we accomplish something or can kick back and relax. However, there are many things we cannot control about our day like being stuck in traffic or the decisions others make which impact our lives. But, we can have a big say in how we will respond to what life sends us.

Enjoyment supersedes happiness in that we consciously decide to make the best of things. Happiness comes and goes with our circumstances. But to enjoy our day necessitates we deliberately practice positive thinking.

A certainty of life is that some day will be our last. Since we don't know when it will come we bring honor to our Creator by making the most of His gift of time. Not only are we brought closer to God but to others too, when we stop enduring and begin enjoying.

Psalm 118:24   LB *This is the day the Lord has made. We will rejoice and be glad in it.*

GOING HIGH ENOUGH TO SEE THE SUN

When my sister came for a visit in cold Canada it was Spring on the calendar but not in our city. Winter weather had stayed beyond its allotted time.

We all know how it is to want to "show off" where you live, to let others see it and love it like you do. We also understand Mother Nature has her own mind and does what she wants. Anyway, the entire time my sister was with us the sun was hidden above the clouds; we were "socked in." On several days we couldn't even see our city's skyline. However, living close to the Rockies allowed us to visit them one day to get a closer look. The view from the bottom was less than ideal so we rode a gondola to the top where it was bitterly cold, but with beautiful sunshine.

Life has many barriers which distort and hinder our view. We often miss the beauty due to the fog and cloud cover of worries, busyness and fatigue. Since we get accustomed to not seeing anything, we tend to forget to keep looking up.

Going high enough to see the SON, no longer hanging on a cross but seated next to the Father is worth whatever you have to do to make it happen. Be assured He has not lost sight of you.

Hebrews 12:2   MEV   *Let us look to Jesus, the author and finisher of our faith, who for the joy that was set before Him endured the cross, despising the shame, and is seated at the right hand of the throne of God.*

SET UP FOR AN UPSET

Super Bowl week captures the attention of millions in North America. The two competing teams are often new to this level of play so it's more difficult to predict who will win. Each team does its best to beat/upset the other. They get into each others' faces trying to intimidate and psych each other out.

Attitude is a huge factor as players bring their skills and experience to the field. Staying positive throughout the entire game is paramount for the victor. You cannot approach a game of this magnitude with doubts or negative thoughts. Each team is preparing to win the game and much of it will be won in the mind before the opening kick-off.

Our lives are similar to a football game. Like a football, life is odd shaped, does not always bounce right and is full of surprises. We are often penalized for small infractions that we did not mean to commit. It just happened. Still, we have to negotiate our way down the field of life, sometimes on offence and other times defense.

Many set themselves up to be upset. They send out signals, verbally and nonverbally, that they can be easily rattled, distracted and defeated. Instead of reprogramming themselves, they expose their emotional buttons which others know just how to push. With this "lack of posture" they are easily "taken out of the game."

Good news is we don't have to live like this. Our Maker did not design us to be frustrated, confused and on edge. We most certainly will be hindered and thrown for losses until we start using His Playbook/Bible, a source that has guided many people from all walks of life to the goal line. Those who run their lives by it will not win every play but are guaranteed to win the game.

Jude 20-21   MSG   *But you, dear friends, carefully build yourselves up in this most holy faith by praying in the Holy Spirit, staying right at the center of God's love, keeping your arms open and outstretched, ready for the mercy of our Master, Jesus Christ. This is the unending life, the real life!*

HEADS UP!

Iwas weed whacking in my back yard along a fence. It was at dusk and the evening breeze felt good coupled with the low humidity of our 3,500 feet elevation. I was almost done when I felt a sharp pain near my lower lip and realized a very upset bee had stung me. Looking up I saw numerous bees buzzing just daring someone to approach. I went the opposite direction and spent the rest of the night with a big fat lip and jaw. Proper medicine finally did its thing, but it still required almost three days for the swelling to subside.

Reflecting on this incident I now realize that had I been looking up, every now and then, I may have avoided disturbing the insect colony. By constantly focusing downward I was totally clueless to any danger until it was too late.

Most "game animals" owe their survival to the art of surveying their surroundings for predators. Their alertness helps them to "live another day." True, they depend on other animals as alarms but they also must remain quite vigilant themselves.

We, who profess the name of Christ, must also be on guard. It's so easy to be absorbed with the immediate challenges that we can become oblivious to the very real threats to our spiritual vitality. The enemy's darts are far more damaging than any bee sting.

Head's up! We are one day closer to His coming!

Mark 13:33 LB *And since you don't know when it will happen, stay alert. Be on the watch for my return*

SPIRITUAL HEALTH

I have discovered that my family has two kinds of hair conditioners: volumizing and nourishing. With my disappearing hairline I am naturally drawn to the volumizing bottle. After all, why not make the best of what you have, right?

After reflecting on my choice, I probably should have chosen the nourishing bottle. Healthy hair serves much better and longer than any volume I may add.

Whether you are a Believer or not, you are definitely a spiritual being. Much of our life is devoted to adding more stuff, to looking good and to keeping up appearances. Our soul can become malnourished in the process and in desperate need of tender loving care from God and others.

We have a choice to add quantity or quality--truth is we need both. Our tendency, however, is to neglect the quality side since it takes longer and we are programmed for instant results.

While I was walking through the men's clothing section of a large department store a saleslady said to me, "You only go through life once. Be good to yourself." My first thought was that she was only trying to get me to buy more. Then I realized the impact of her statement. More is not always better--go for quality.

Only our spirit will survive this life on earth so we must do all we can to take care of it. Live long and be in spiritual health.

Jeremiah 29:11 NKJV *For I know the thoughts that I think toward you, says the LORD, thoughts of peace and not of evil, to give you a future and a hope.*

HOPE

Paul, author of much of the New Testament, writes, "And now these three remain: faith, hope and love." No one disputed the importance of love, but *hope* is not all that bad either. In fact, we are powerless without it. The disciples' faith got a bump after the resurrection. To personally see Christ risen had to put a new spring in their steps.

All of us need a shot of hope. It has been said, "Without hope in the future there is no power in the present." Going on vacation or getting ready to do something special energizes you. Your strength and stamina rise above normal. You find yourself attacking your "to do list" rather than avoiding it. Unfortunately, many Believers act like they have no hope which is a big turnoff for non-Christians.

Life can be tough at times and we don't always feel hopeful, especially when everything seems uphill. A slogan that has helped me is: "Hope is Holding On Praying Expectantly."

This describes where most of us live. We are holding on to our faith and confidence that God really is in control.

Regularly reading the book of hope (Bible), hanging out on purpose with hopeful, positive people and reducing negative input from the media could literally save your life.

Romans 5:3-5 Phillips *"This doesn't mean, of course, that we have only a hope of future joys—we can be full of joy here and now even in our trials and troubles. Taken in the right spirit these very things will give us patient endurance; this in turn will develop a mature character, and a character of this sort produces a steady hope, a hope that will never disappoint us. Already we have some experience of the love of God flooding through our hearts by the Holy Spirit given to us."*

MISCOMMUNICATION

My wife and I were in the car on our way to attend an "important" Christmas banquet. It was to be a grand evening meeting new people and colleagues in our "new city." We had the address and allowed enough travel time but, after searching for over an hour, we discovered our information was incorrect. Since we didn't have a name for the venue and all the people who knew about the party were at the party, we found ourselves all dressed up with no place to go.

This scenario probably happens to most of us sooner or later. It was no one's fault-just miscommunication. Omission of details can mislead and derail good intentions. Because we can do so many things we tend to overdo and glitches happen.

You have to be impressed when reading the Christmas story of the great use of detail given to the shepherds and Wise Men. God spoke their language: angels to those guarding the flocks and a star to people who studied the heavens. Precise information helped people find the Savior.

Those of us who know very well the biblical account of Christ's coming must be careful that we communicate it accurately to others who don't know. We cannot assume that others comprehend the simplicity of finding Jesus. Many get lost along the way when vital details are omitted.

What a great opportunity we have to direct friends and family to the One who invented Christmas. Better yet--take them with you since you know the way!

Luke 2:17-18   LB *The shepherds told everyone what had happened and what the angel had said to them about this child. All who heard the shepherds' story expressed astonishment.*

HOW DO YOU TREAT LITTLE PEOPLE?

I will define "Little People" as those who cannot do any-thing for you like advance your career or make you look better. (They might be employees behind counters, mainte-nance personnel, or even handicapped individuals.) If not careful, we can pay more attention to the "helper dog" and literally ignore the person in the wheelchair.

But, it is even more subtle and insidious than the previ-ously named people. Technology allows more immediate communication than ever, but we often choose to ignore e-mails or texts or calls.

Now, prioritizing our time is important. We all employ "gatekeepers" of some kind--either a person who guards our schedule or by our own avoidance of communicating with someone who contacted us in good faith. The fallout can be devastating for everyone. The person who wants to connect with you can interpret your lack of response as meaning you lack care. All of this leads to discouragement, and they may judge you more harshly than you know. Your integrity is in question and relationships are often terminated even though this is not what you intended.

On the other hand, "What goes around comes around." Understand, God is keeping the records; He deeply cares how we treat all people, especially "little ones."

Over and over scripture clearly shows how Jesus cared for folks others despised or did not see. Lepers, blind and lame people, the mentally ill: all of these humans were special to the Master.

We can all improve in this matter. Think about it.

Matthew 25:40 MSG *Then the King will say, 'I'm telling the solemn truth: Whenever you did one of these things to someone overlooked or ignored, that was me—you did it to me.'*

RESIGNATION

In our "western culture" resignation often has a negative connotation. The idea of quitting or adopting a submissive posture seems weak to many. We are programmed to "hang in there", to "go the distance" and to persevere. This conditioning is not without merit for you need these qualities to accomplish much in this world.

But, in God's economy, the playing ground is different and many miss the point. It is His intent that we willfully surrender to His lead and rule--to resign ourselves to His will. This is not an easy proposition: trusting someone whom we have never seen.

God will never force us to acquiesce to His guidance and control--we must do it deliberately in a tangible fashion. This is not a "one time fits all plan" but a lifestyle of deference to Higher Intent.

The good news is that living in such a manner actually causes us to Re-Sign to a whole new life of opportunity and challenge. Proper vertical alignment will greatly enhance our horizontal relationships.

1 Peter 2:21 NLT *For God called you to do good, even if it means suffering, just as Christ suffered for you. He is your example, and you must follow in His steps.*

HOW YA DOIN', COACH?

The USA is a sports-crazed nation. The term "coach" has replaced designations like mentor, example and supervisor. Exposure to coaches from all kinds of sports teams has filtered into our business world as leaders are encouraged to employ coaching techniques in the workplace.

Each of us is a coach to someone whether we intend to be or not. There is a person or group of people who are looking to you for help and direction. So, how do you become a coach? What does a coach do?

I received an invitation to attend a seminar on coaching skills for managers and supervisors. The brochure revealed a little on what would be taught. Consider these suggestions as you look over "the team" God has placed in your life:

Recognize and Utilize Talent. This is a major function of a coach, not to dwell on someone's weaknesses but to focus on what they do well. How ya doin', coach?

Generate The Desire to Win. It is no accident that some coaches win more than they lose. They have learned how to create and maintain a winning atmosphere. If they fail, they fail forward. How ya doin', coach?

End Mediocrity. High expectations of others is vital if we're to lift them above average. Think about a teacher or someone who challenged you to "step up". They expected more from you and you were the better for it. How ya doin', coach?

Redirect The Problem Person. A coach knows that potential is often covered up by unresolved or neglected problems. God has uniquely gifted you to help someone get on the right track. How ya doin', coach?

Inspire Teamwork. Getting diverse people to work and communicate together has never been easy. Whether it be your family or coworkers or a group you're in, it's worth your investment to inspire them to win together rather that lose separately. How ya doin'...Coach?

1 Corinthians 11:1 LB *And you should follow my example, just as I follow Christ's.*

SEAT OCCUPIED

Several years ago a good friend took me to see the Memorial Museum in Oklahoma City where hundreds of innocent people, from small children to aging grandparents, lost their lives when the downtown federal building was blown up. Our on-site visit revealed twenty square blocks were affected by the blast. Over 200 buildings were damaged, 140 totally destroyed, several of which were historic churches. The bombing killed 168 people and more than 680 others were injured.

There were nine tiered rows of empty chairs out on the lawn--one for each victim. Walking through the museum a reverent hush was evident as visitors quietly paid their respect. Even the volunteer guides spoke of the tragedy in a soft, reverent manner, holding back the tears.

At Easter we commemorate another tragedy that turned triumphant. Jesus was unfairly tried and executed. But, three days later another blast occurred which has impacted the whole world. This time the seat is occupied by our Savior who sits at the right hand of the Father as our lawyer. He invites you to be a client.

Hebrews 10:12   LB *But Christ gave himself to God for our sins as one sacrifice for all time and then sat down in the place of highest honor at God's right hand...*

HURRY

Christmas--so much to do, so much to buy and so many places to be. A sign in my office reads, "I must hurry for there they go and I am their leader." So easy to feel like everyone is passing us, making better time or accomplishing more than we are!

Not true! Oh, some will always advance more quickly than we do. But, for the most part, most of us are in the same boat, struggling with doing too much too quickly which causes us to rush. It's in this "hurry" stage where we lose our peace and compound our problems.

Counteracting our hurry is never easy. Old habits are familiar and comfortable--they seem right. Intentional "slow down" tactics must be employed if we're to "smell the flowers" of the Christmas season.

One tactic is to simplify our lives by doing only the essential items on our "to do lists." They are the ones you do during an emergency. It's amazing how quickly our schedule sorts out when an emergency comes our way. Things we thought were so important now fade as more critical matters surface.

The Christmas story is read and dramatized thousands of times each year. This great event did not come hurriedly. The prolific writer Saint Paul said that Christ came to earth "in the fullness of time." This means everything was planned, arrangements had been made and God's eternal plan was on time.

Enjoy your Christmas this year in the slower lane; it will allow you to enjoy the holiday pace.

Galatians 4:4   AMP   *But when the proper time had fully come, God sent His Son, born of a woman, born subject to [the regulations of] the Law...*

IGNORING ALARMS

Most families run on the clock. Getting up in the morning is not easy. Alarm clock manufacturers are constantly striving to improve their products promising "fool proof" devices that are sure to work on the soundest sleeper. And so we buy this "new and improved" technology to jump start ourselves or a family member. Usually they work for a while and we relax. But then comes the day when the alarm goes on and on waking the entire household except the in-tended receiver. What went wrong with our "cure-all-clock"?

Well, the alarm is not at fault--it does what it was designed to do. However, the receiver began ignoring the wake-up call, to let it go on longer before responding. Each time the re-sponse time is lengthened the effectiveness of the alarm is di-minished.

There are numerous alarms which go off in our lives on a regular basis. We tend to choose which ones to ignore. One which we dare not avoid is the Spirit of God talking to us.

It's that still, small voice which says we shouldn't act a certain way or follow through on what we're thinking. This alarm is never intended to hurt us but only to help. However, like an alarm clock it can be ignored by our own free will.

Getting a late start can mess up your entire day. Ignoring God's call can change your destiny.

Revelation 3:20 LB *"Look! I have been standing at the door, and I am constantly knocking. If anyone hears me calling him and opens the door, I will come in and fellowship with him and he with me."*

SHELF LIFE

Shelf life has become a household word. It refers to how long an item can maintain its quality and potential while remaining on a shelf. One report, probably debatable, indicates a Twinkie has a shelf life of 20 years. At any rate, we regularly use things which have been stored for some time and we expect them to perform, work or even taste good. Manufacturers have added preservatives of one kind or another to insure this long term usability.

Closer to home, most of us experience times of "shelf life" where we find ourselves on hold, waiting to be active and "doing our thing" again. These times can be precipitated by health problems, career changes and other family situations. It is very challenging to return to the shelf once you have been active and involved. Nevertheless, shelf life is a part of living and so we need to make the most of it.

You will not find the term "shelf life" in the Bible but the concept is there. As you reflect on Psalm 23, consider these phrases: *"He leadeth me beside the still waters." "He restoreth my soul."* Depletion of our energies and resources is quite common and so we need "time-outs", to be renewed and to regroup. While on the shelf God wants to touch us, to slow us down so we can rearrange our priorities and to assure a useful future.

When you go on the shelf don't look at it as down time or failure. It can be a gift from the Shepherd for even greater success in the future.

Psalm 23:1-3 NLV *The Lord is my Shepherd. I will have everything I need. He lets me rest in fields of green grass. He leads me beside the quiet waters. He makes me strong again. He leads me in the way of living right with Himself which brings honor to His name.*

SHELF TALK

We all go through times when we're on the shelf. Whether it be physical, relational, marital, emotional or financial issues we are facing, the question is, "What do we say to ourselves when we're on the shelf?"

Shelf talk always accompanies "shelf life." We believe our own voice more than any other. So, when you verbally or subconsciously tell yourself things like, "I'm a failure" or "I'm no good" or "I'm washed up" or "There's no hope" you can literally sabotage your future.

Faith would have us speak encouragingly to ourselves. Some phrases that have and continue to help me are:

This Too Shall Pass. My mother has immeasurably helped me with this one. It is an affirming statement of hope in an all-caring God who sees me and has grace to assist me no matter what comes my way. It says, "Hold on, the story is not over; the best is still to come."

Keep Looking Up. Our outlook varies according to how we feel and the changing environment we encounter. When we look up we realize we're not alone--God is right beside us.

I'm One Of God's Favorite Kids. Someone has said the reason God constantly watches over us is He can't take his eyes off of us. My songwriter friend describes it this way: "He Loves Me Like I Was His Only Child…". When we're on the shelf we tend to feel forgotten as life passes us by. Remember, the slower pace of the shelf allows us more time to enjoy the fellowship of our heavenly Father if we want.

Keep Looking Up! This Too Shall Pass! You're One Of God's Favorites!

Joshua 1:9 NLV *Have I not told you? Be strong and have strength of heart! Do not be afraid or lose faith. For the Lord your God is with you anywhere you go.*

THE ROOT CAUSE

I lived for over half of a century before experiencing my first root canal. Pain killers and other remedies help for a while but other than pulling a valuable tooth, only a root canal can solve a root problem.

We live in a world where quick and easy fixes are not only wanted but deemed necessary by many. Whether it be winning the lottery to solve our financial pressures or divorce to eliminate our marital struggles, people continually look for ways out of their dilemmas.

According to my dentist, 55% of people in the USA do not practice regular health care. They deal with symptoms primarily by purchasing over the counter medicines.

When we ignore or deny real issues and only respond to them on a surface level the difficulties tend to get worse, not better. This approach allows our problems to get on top of us rather than our being on top of them. Many maladies are treatable if caught in time, but we must be honest about our situation.

Spiritual problems are no exception. Attitude adjustments, positive thinking, confession, going to church and counselling are all legitimate ways to draw closer to God. But the root cause may be our heart. If there is rebellion and sin then we need the Great Physician to operate, to clean out blocked arteries which sap our very life and joy.

As you hurry through another week, consider your life and all the stuff you're dealing with. Root cause therapy is worth the price you have to pay for it.

Proverbs 4:23 NLT *Guard your heart above all else for it determines the course of your life.*

IGNORNING RADAR

I'm a fan of nature shows. It fascinates me to see how God has created animals with all their inherent survival abilities. Each species is unique and perfectly adapted to its environment.

In one show the subject was bats--not one of my favorites. Researchers were capturing bats for tagging and monitoring. They employed a simple net strung from the trees near known dwelling places of bats.

One statement caught my attention: "Even though bats are equipped with built-in radar they often ignore using it when flying through familiar places." The only way these super sensitive animals can be caught is when they disregard their God-given instincts and fly directly into the net.

As born again believers, we have been given spiritual radar from our Creator God, through His Holy Spirit. We can move safely through the traps of our world as long as we listen to the voice of God which comes to us via scripture, anointed preaching and teaching, and from those who are close to us. When we "fly on" and ignore our internal warnings, then we are subject to being caught in the snares of this world.

Like bats, we tend to let our guard down around the familiar. That's why so many auto accidents happen so close to home--we just don't expect it. Each time we fail to heed the warnings we become more susceptible to the traps of our enemy. Unlike the benevolent scientists, Satan wants to destroy us. Stay alert!

Ephesians 5:15-17 LB *So be careful how you act; these are difficult days. Don't be fools; be wise: make the most of every opportunity you have for doing good. Don't act thoughtlessly, but try to find out and do whatever the Lord wants you to.*

IN YOUR ELEMENT

My family had fun visiting the Oregon Coast Aquarium, ranked in the top ten best aquariums in the world. Marine life is so fascinating for there is much we don't know about the ocean's inhabitants.

My favorite part is the sea lions and seals. These land and sea creatures have their own area of water and land formations in which to swim. Up on the rocks they are quite awkward and unsteady. But once they go in the water they become peaceful and carefree in their movement. They swim upside down as easily as right side up. With only a stroke or two of their fins/arms they are propelled like a torpedo. I find myself somewhat envious of their "stress free" environment.

Sometimes we find ourselves operating out of our comfort zone on rocky, uneven terrain. Our low performance is rather predictable as we fumble and stumble our way through another day or assignment--we are definitely out of our element. True, at times we are forced to maneuver and function in situations which are not conducive to our personality or preferences and that's life. But it is natural to want to be in your element, to maximize your talents and to diminish your stress load. Nothing wrong with desiring peace by withdrawing from some "urgent" appointments for a time of relaxation and fun.

Staying in your element is a lifelong process. However, this is not to suggest shirking your duty or neglecting your obligations. Our Lord was very much out of His element when he walked this Earth; yet, He modelled for us a blueprint for success to his mission: time alone and time with his Father. These two simple habits made him a thermostat and not a thermometer.

As much as you can, stay in your element. Your world will improve if you do.

1 Corinthians 12:11 LB I*t is the same and only Holy Spirit who gives all these gifts and powers, deciding which each one of us should have.*

INCREASING YOUR THANKFULNESS

I have always loved Thanksgiving. As a kid growing up it was a great time to be with family, have fun and enjoy delicious food. I'm sure my enjoyment was enhanced because I did not have to purchase or prepare the meal.

It is good to be thankful for God's blessings, to have a day when we purposely celebrate our good fortune. But time races on and Christmas decorations appear before our carved pumpkins lose their shape.

Ideally we should be thankful all the time--scripture tells us to do so and that's good. Taking our blessings for granted is something we all do too much. Being reminded that I am blessed to live in freedom, to have food and shelter, and to not fear my future is priceless.

Increasing our thankfulness is necessary because we pro-gressively become desensitized to our blessings. We can even believe they are owed to us by God and others. When we assume this kind of thinking we become less Christlike. Our humanity suffers and the gulf between the "haves" and "have nots" gets bigger.

- To increase your thankfulness, consider the following action steps:
- Next time you look in the mirror thank God you are alive and can see.
- Find something good in everyone you meet and sincerely compliment them if possible.
- Realize you are more loved than you know.
- Slow down long enough to reflect and revel in the beautiful world God created.
- Do something intentional to help someone in need.
- Take a little longer to thank God for your food and family.
- Deny yourself something so you can focus on what you have rather than what you want.

Thanks living is a great way to spend your days.

Colossians 3:15   MSG   *Let the peace of Christ keep you in tune with each other, in step with each other. None of this going off and doing your own thing. And cultivate thankfulness.*

IT'S ALL HOW YOU LOOK AT IT

After taking my girls to school one day I returned home to discover I didn't have my house keys. No problem! I just used my garage door opener. As I walked into the garage our new kitten ran and hid behind the freezer.

Now, I'm not a cat lover but this one really was a cute fur ball. Seeing the tiny pet cowering under the coils of the freezer caused me to wonder how things look from a kitty's perspective. We must all look like giants to a creature whose eyes are no more than four inches off the ground. We'd be frightened too if we were so small.

Many people view life from a limited perspective. Like the old Technicolor movies which had a wide view but not much height or depth, we often miss the "big picture" and only see what is just around us. Our view can be distorted causing us to see people or things bigger than they really are. Such distortion may cause us to run and hide like the kitten.

Ground level viewing can come from low self-esteem or our refusal to grow up in Christ and take on the responsibilities maturity demands. The main complication is leaving God out of our sight. When He is omitted, we tend to walk by "fright" rather than by faith.

Remember: Your Owner loves you and wants you to sense all the dimensions of His care.

Ephesians 3:17-19 NLT   *Then Christ will make His home in your hearts as you trust in Him. Your roots will grow down into God's love and keep you strong. And may you have the power to understand, as all God's people should, how wide, how long, how high, and how deep His love is. May you experience the love of Christ, though it is too great to understand fully. Then you will be made complete with all the fullness of life and power that comes from God.*

LET IT GO

Okay--life is full of battles and challenges. Anyone worth their salt has learned that we win some and lose some but we stay in the game. However, we tend to get overextended, at times, and run out of fingers to plug the holes and prevent the dam from bursting. Dealing with too many issues at the same time spells defeat. So, we have to let some things go either by choice or by force, the latter to be avoided if possible.

No doubt someone has said to you "Let it go!" At first this may sound like bad advice since we may perceive it as failure or cowardice. On the contrary, it's usually good counsel for you have to be selective to be effective in life's campaign.

Rock sculptors know just what to chip away in order to produce a statue or other work of art. It is in the deletion that freedom and beauty comes. Likewise, much of what we deal with day by day is excess baggage which only drains our limited resources.

"Let it go" for real by giving it to God. He's up 24/7 anyway so why not let Him handle it? He's never lost a battle. Go with the WINNER!

Philippians 3:13 LB *No, dear brothers, I am still not all I should be, but I am bringing all my energies to bear on this one thing: Forgetting the past and looking forward to what lies ahead.*

STAND BY

There are many kinds of tickets you can purchase to fly on a commercial airplane. The most economical is "stand by" which basically means if there's still room after everyone has boarded you will be permitted to travel.

This works okay most of the time but not so much at Christmas. My daughter was stuck for many hours in Salt Lake City, trying to get to her family in Calgary.

Waiting in an airport is not pleasant. Getting "bumped" is no great honor. But there is something far more important: Do you have the right ticket to go to heaven? Good news! It has already been paid for by Christ on the cross. All we have to do is "buy in" to a personal relationship with the Savior.

Many, I suspect, are hoping to make their final flight with a "stand-by" ticket. They look like a passenger; they have documents which indicate they plan to fly (baptism, church membership, good deeds); but when final boarding is announced, they miss the flight because no one lands in Heaven on "stand-by." All of this can be changed when you know the Pilot.

Acts 3:19 MSG *Now it's time to change your ways! Turn to face God so He can wipe away your sins, pour out showers of blessing to refresh you, and send you the Messiah He prepared for you, namely, Jesus.*

IT'S EASY TO FORGET

Memory can be both a blessing and a curse. We all have past events we would like to erase from our mental hard drive.

Along with the bad there is much good as we've stored up wonderful sights, sounds, smells and sensations which bring us pleasure and delight. Special days can be relived over and over because our mind has recorded them.

Remembering is often difficult but it's easy to forget. One date we dare not forget is 9-11-01, a tragic day that changed our world. Such a day of infamy requires civilized people to remember on purpose.

May we never forget that life is precious and precarious. All of us are terminal--we're not getting out of this world alive.

Also don't forget that into such a world Jesus came. He wants to take us to a terrorist-free paradise. Got your ticket?

Deuteronomy. 8:11 MSG *Make sure you don't forget GOD, your God, by not keeping His commandments, His rules and regulations that I command you today.*

LESSONS FROM THE FIRE

I had accepted a call to pastor a great church in Alberta, Canada. We were driving to Calgary when, all of a sudden and out of nowhere, smoke started coming out of the trunk of our car. We pulled to the median on the freeway and quickly exited the vehicle. A passing motorist called 9-1-1 and we waited for help to come. We were out in the "middle of nowhere."

As my family and I stood under the hot Montana sun, we experienced God's protecting grace and mercy as we watched our car burn while we were totally unharmed. Police and firemen arrived and as the smoke cleared lessons began to surface:

1. Life is unfair but God is always good.

2. Things can be replaced but not people.

3. God has "His people" strategically placed to reassure us that He is involved in our lives, especially when bad things happen. Our firemen were Christians who sang on the weekends as a gospel quartet.

4. When the heat is on, you quickly find out what your priorities are. My wife's Bible was saved from the flames in the back window.

5. When you experience a tragedy, you discover you have more loving friends than you ever dreamed.

6. A "close call" is a wake-up call for all of us.

7. Danger can be lurking so close and yet you are unaware. It pays to be ready to meet your Maker.

8. Life's losses make us more sensitive to the plight of others. When I see problems on the highway I am compelled to pray even harder for the victims and first responders.

9. There are some things we'll never understand in this life even though a cause is given. The official cause of our fire was a short in a tail light.

10. The Devil meant it to sidetrack us, but God specializes in preventing derailment.

Genesis 50:20a NLT *You intended to harm me, but God intended it all for good.*

IT'S GONNA MAKE A GOOD STORY

I do not know what your idea of heaven is. Of course there is much speculation of what we'll do or not do. I believe one of the highlights will be to swap stories with family and friends about how God brought us through this world to be with Him forever.

One chapter we will not want to omit is how He saved us. Everyone's story will be a little different but surprisingly the same. We will want to honor those who played a significant role in our coming to Christ like a grandparent or teacher.

There will be those people we can count on one hand that influenced us for God and for good. With our minds uninhibited by forgetfulness we will remember those we forgot: people who were with us at the right time, encouraging and reminding us to keep looking up, pressing forward and not to quit. In eternity we will have unlimited time to say thanks and celebrate with others who made the biggest and best decision of their lives to invite Jesus into their hearts.

Whatever you're going through right now will make a good story someday as you recall all the miracles which should not have happened and yet did. We'll also hear stories not included in sacred writ which the Apostles and Patriarchs will personally share. It's gonna be great!

Don't miss the "neverending story" of God's great care and love. See you there!

2 Samuel 22:3 LB *I will hide in God, Who is my rock and my refuge. He is my shield and my salvation, My refuge and high tower. Thank you, O my Savior, for saving me from all my enemies.*

MAKE LIFE EASIER FOR EVERYBODY

I had just come through the checkout of a large department store when I heard a cashier supervisor say to a group of employees, "Make life easier for everybody." The intent of his remark was to encourage his team to lighten up and be cooperative.

You don't have to live too long to realize life is sometimes hard. Everyone you meet is going through some kind of challenge with health, finances, marital struggles, kid problems, you name it. We cannot change their situation or live their lives for them. But, we can make their day go a little better by our disposition and attitude. This is never easy and we will need God's help to sustain this behavior.

There are many ways we can enhance the quality of life for someone else. Let's look at a few:

Smile. Body language speaks loudly and communicates positive feelings in others.

Courtesy. "Please" and "thank you" are still magic words which we don't hear enough, even around home.

Tone of Voice. Fifty-five percent of people's perception of us comes from our tone of voice. We all can make positive changes.

RSVP. In this day of cell phones, e-mails, texts and Instagrams we often neglect to get back with people letting them know we got their message or invitation. This causes unnecessary stress and strains relationships.

Prayer. We tend to not fully appreciate the power of prayer but that does not diminish its effectiveness. Many of the interpersonal problems we deal with could be resolved if we spent extra time praying for a person or situation. Give it a try!

Ephesians 4:32   MSG   *Be gentle with one another, sensitive. Forgive one another as quickly and thoroughly as God in Christ forgave you.*

PLAYING KEEP-A-WAY

Like many North American parents, I have spent my fair share of time watching my kids play organized sports. Attending one of my daughter's early softball games I noticed how challenging it was for the players to get the ball back to the pitcher.

As the game progresses fatigue and apathy can develop. The catcher's throw is often in the dirt which necessitates an infielder snagging the ball and throwing it back to the mound. Occasionally it requires several throws to actually get the ball back to the pitcher's mitt.

Observing this "keep it away from the pitcher" phenomena, prompted me to think how this kind of activity occurs in the game of life. We throw the ball over someone's head or make them work harder to retrieve our pitch that's in the dirt. In other words, we fail to work as a team by lack of follow through and inattention to detail.

We wonder why the opposition is hitting the ball past us--it must be the pitcher's fault. Yet we wear out our co-workers and, sometimes, friends chasing errant throws. The momentum of the game changes, and runs are scored against us simply because we do not work or minister as a team. Sadly, many talented players are lost as they give up in frustration.

All of us have daily opportunities to assist those we live, play and work with. Let us not work against each other. The only way to win is to win together.

1 Corinthians 12:21-22   LB *The eye can never say to the hand, "I don't need you." The head can't say to the feet, "I don't need you." And some of the parts that seem weakest and least important are really the most necessary.*

IT'S JUST A SQUIRREL

On January 2nd of this new millennium, I was standing in our Family Life Center talking to our Sunday School Superintendent. I had just made the statement, "Well, it looks like we made it through Y2K." (There was widespread fear that when the calendar changed to 2000, something cataclysmic might happen.)

All of a sudden our power went off. Many thoughts went through our heads since we all had been programmed to expect millennial problems. Within seconds another member, who had been looking out a window across the parking lot, saw a puff of smoke emitted from a nearby electrical transformer which literally robbed 5000 customers of electricity for two plus hours. Our early suspicion that a wayward squirrel had triggered the outage was later confirmed by the power company technicians. We went ahead with our worship service with no power or light but only some candles.

As I reflect back on that day many interesting things come to mind. Some people came in late and actually thought the Y2K bug had struck. One cannot blame them for thinking so with all the conditioning of the previous months. It was not until someone told them what happened that they stopped believing the worst. How like human nature it is for us to know the truth and assume everyone else knows what we know or to not know what's going on and remain in the dark by not asking.

Many times in our lives, it really is "just a squirrel," not the end of the world or some sinister plot against our way of living or even someone trying to mess up our lives. It's just life--something wandered into the wrong space and disrupted our agenda. We who follow Christ know that the Devil tries to destabilize and distract us in any way he can. It's easy to give him more credit than he deserves as though he is under every rock along our path.

Our Maker wants us to think and be observant. Many problems in life are the result of a bad decision--yours or that of someone else. Yes, we live in a world of cause and effect but our Lord is with us no matter what. Keep looking up!

Isaiah 41:10 GNT *Do not be afraid—I am with you! I am your God—let nothing terrify you! I will make you strong and help you; I will protect you and save you.*

LIFE IS FULL OF PICKING

My wife and I went berry picking for Saskatoons, a popular fruit in Western Canada. It is slightly smaller than a blueberry and tastes wonderful, especially when baked in a pie.

As we filled our pails at the u-pick farm, the morning sun was on its way up and the bees and birds were buzzing and chirping. The bushes, about 5-6 feet high, were loaded with fruit but most of the ripe berries were already picked or located deeper into the interior of the farm. So, you had to be selective in order to secure the ripe ones and not damage the berries "still in process."

Life is full of picking. We constantly make choices about what to gather and what to leave, which is good and which is best, between grabbing and gently plucking. These choices are almost automatic unless we deliberately take time to consider their impact on us and others.

For example, I can choose to cause others to relate to me on my terms rather than try to understand their way of thinking. I can go for what I want and totally disregard the maturing process in others, expecting them to either go along with me or be spoiled.

Our Creator has given us the wonderful gift of choice. Certainly, choosing to follow Christ is one of life's greatest blessings. But, it is in our moment by moment "picking" that we can harm or hinder. Select carefully and tenderly--so many are depending on it.

Deuteronomy 30:19 LB *I call heaven and earth to witness against you that today I have set before you life or death, blessing or curse. Oh, that you would choose life; that you and your children might live!*

SHIELDED

One Sunday night I was riding with a pastor friend and his wife. We had just pulled out on the highway when someone from a passing car threw a rock and hit our windshield on the driver's side. Had we been going any faster this "missile" would probably have penetrated the glass and struck the driver. After we stopped for a moment to recover from our "close call" we thanked God for His protection.

Scripture describes God as being our "shield." Just like the see-through glass covering the dashboard of our car, we tend to look past the everyday mercies of the Lord. Only heaven will reveal the numerous times we should have been hurt or even killed but God had a different plan and we were spared.

Like in safety glass, God has many built-in protections for us. Be reminded of His care and pray for others as they travel.

Oh yes, we also prayed for the "rock throwers" that they would come to their senses and stop their foolish behavior.

Psalm 91:1-4 NKJV *He who dwells in the secret place of the Most High Shall abide under the shadow of the Almighty. I will say of the LORD, "He is my refuge and my fortress; My God, in Him I will trust." Surely He shall deliver you from the snare of the fowler and from the perilous pestilence. He shall cover you with His feathers, and under His wings you shall take refuge; His truth shall be your shield and buckler.*

THE VIEW FROM ABOVE

Surrounded by some new friends, I had the privilege of viewing a magnificent North American city from a 600-foot high revolving restaurant. Objects that appeared so big on the ground now looked small. Places which were obscure at street level were now easily seen. As night relieved the day, the darkness brought a whole new beauty to the city, one of awe rather than dread.

All of us, from time to time, need to go up higher to view "our world" above the routines of life. It's so easy to get bogged down with our daily stresses that we tend to lose perspective. Going up higher does not have to be a physical elevation but can be anything wholesome which lifts our spirits, renews our dreams and causes us to think creatively. A concert, a walk in the woods or on the beach, time spent with "big thinkers," all of these have elevating potential.

Let us not forget our Lord's example--He often withdrew from the crowd to go up on the hillsides and pray. Talking to our Heavenly Father is the ultimate elevator.

Psalm 73:28 LB   *But as for me, I get as close to Him as I can! I have chosen Him, and I will tell everyone about the wonderful ways He rescues me.*

LIFE IS LIKE A DRAWING

Dennis the Menace's mother was looking over her son's shoulder as he created a picture. Dennis explaining, "I won't know what I'm drawing until I'm finished."

We all are in the midst of a life drawing and it's unclear how the final product will look. True, we have our one and five year plans but so much happens in the meantime. Unfortunately, we do not control many things which impact our lives like the sin and poor judgment of others or a heredity disease which preys upon our particular gene mix. At times it seems like a beautiful picture is being developed and then the unexpected happens and our creation reverts to a blur.

Although no artist, I know it usually takes many colors to make a painting. It would be great to have all bright shades full of sparkle and hope. But, often darker colors form the foundation and undertones of the artist's drawing. The muted strokes allow lighter colors to be more pronounced and vivid, resulting in a balanced and proportional view of some scene or person.

Good news! God is able to see the entire canvas of our life. We may not be able to make sense of anything when all the while He's making something that will last forever.

We must stay flexible, submit to His choice of materials and keep on drawing strength from Him. In His time, we will be suitable for framing.

1 Corinthians. 13:12 NIV *For now we see only a reflection as in a mirror; then we shall see face to face. Now I know in part; then I shall know fully, even as I am fully known.*

MEASURING SUCCESS

We live in a world where performance is constantly measured. This is proper to do for improvement is negated if we don't know how we're currently doing.

The downside of measuring is in the instruments used. So much of what we accomplish is intrinsic; in other words, one cannot calibrate intent or concern or compassion. These fly under the radar and often go unnoticed.

When my wife and I were missionaries in Kenya, we became quite discouraged after living there for about a year. Coming from our "Western World" where success is judged by stats, we felt like nothing was happening in our ministry, that we were losers.

One of our church members, a brilliant man with a PhD from the USA, listened to us as we shared how we felt. I'll never forget his words of wisdom. He said, "You've stayed with us for a year and you have loved us. We count that as success."

The phrase "God is keeping the record" is so true. He sees our heart and motive. His mode of measuring us is so superior to any earthly device.

Be encouraged! Sometimes the best we can offer is simply to hang in there with someone and love them through it. You're probably more of a success story than you know.

John 3:27 a MSG *It's not possible for a person to succeed—I'm talking about eternal success—without heaven's help*

LIVING BEYOND YOUR MEANS

We live in a world that stretches all of us. Our plans and dreams can evaporate so quickly leaving us bewildered and confused. Reality is like a gravitational force which pulls us down with less than a soft landing. We can even begin to question the purpose for our existence.

Most of us have been programmed to "live within our means." In other words, to manage our resources and adjust our lifestyle so that income and outgo are somewhat equal. Credit can cause these two entities to get out of balance as we try to provide for our family needs and cope with daily pressures. We are proud of ourselves and admire others when comfortable living is achieved. Those who consistently live otherwise are looked down upon, even excluded from some circles.

But, there is a dimension wherein "living beyond your means" is not only expected but normal--our spiritual walk with God. Faith, if anything, is living beyond your means.

Because it is so counter to our physical world it is not easy to practice. Yet, if you and I are to please God we must follow and obey Him whether it is financially sound or not.

Our heroes in scripture lived this way and we celebrate them. They were misunderstood by their contemporaries and we may be too.

Bottom line. Do your best to stay balanced, and if you err, do so on the side of faith.

Mark 12:42-44 MSG *Sitting across from the offering box, he was observing how the crowd tossed money in for the collection. Many of the rich were making large contributions. One poor widow came up and put in two small coins—a measly two cents. Jesus called his disciples over and said, "The truth is that this poor widow gave more to the collection than all the others put together. All the others gave what they'll never miss; she gave extravagantly what she couldn't afford—she gave her all."*

NO MAN'S LAND

While driving my daughters to school one day I noticed some very tall grass covering one corner of an intersection in an upscale neighborhood. Homeowners there were known for their neatly manicured lawns. In fact, on both sides of the unmown grass the properties were immaculate.

It appeared the respective residents stopped mowing at their property line and allowed the corner to grow unattended.

This "no man's land" provides an interesting commentary on human nature. Having driven by several times left me with some impressions:

- This eyesore could be easily avoided if the adjacent neighbors mowed a little beyond their property line.
- The entire community suffers and looks worse because of this neglect.

- This one negative piece of ground diminishes the beauty of the surrounding homes. We tend to miss the good yards and focus on the one bad spot.

We encounter this type of "who's supposed to do it" attitude every day. No wonder Jesus told us to do more than is expected, especially in our relationships with others. Second mile living allows others to see the positive, lifts morale and self-worth, and makes God's neighborhood more beautiful.

Matthew 5:38-42 MSG *Here's another old saying that deserves a second look: 'Eye for eye, tooth for tooth'. Is that going to get us anywhere? Here's what I propose: 'Don't hit back at all.' If someone strikes you, stand there and take it. If someone drags you into court and sues for the shirt off your back, giftwrap your best coat and make a present of it. And if someone takes unfair advantage of you, use the occasion to practice the servant life. No more tit-for-tat stuff. Live generously.*

SOMEBODY'S GOTTA MOVE

After a 75-minute delay I finally boarded the airplane to go home. My flight attendant was having a bad day and it showed. An elderly gentleman told the attendant he could not find his seat in the back so he sat down next to me in the front row. Her response to him was less than kind. Finally, the last passenger arrived, and we were ready to taxi except there was a weight distribution problem in this regional size jet. The announcement was made for someone in the first four rows to move to the back so the plane could be balanced. I found myself the lone volunteer. As I got up and moved to the back, much to my surprise the entire plane load of passengers clapped and cheered.

Life is full of opportunities to make things better. It usually involves giving up something in order to achieve the next level. This is true in relationships, careers, athletics or whatever. Reflections from my flight include:

- Flexibility is a rewarding asset. Not only was my move appreciated by fellow travelers, but I actually ended up in a better seat with no one next to me so more comfort.

- Moving to the back seemed to ease the "cabin pressure" and the flight attendant started smiling. We often hold the key to others having a better day.

- Our actions do make an impact. All who fly have their "horror stories," and they usually involve rudeness by someone. As I departed the escalator at the airport, a lady went out of her way to thank me for giving up my seat.

- Giving up can become a way of life. It must be practiced in order to feel normal. My little gesture was not heroic or saintly but simply a matter of choice.

Bottom line: Jesus gave up so we could ultimately go up. Let us never forget this.

Romans 12:10 MSG *Love from the center of who you are; don't fake it. Run for dear life from evil; hold on for dear life to good. Be good friends who love deeply; practice playing second fiddle.*

NOT ONE MINUTE LONGER...

While driving my car one day I heard a radio talk show host say, "Don't waste one minute longer hating." This statement captured my attention for we do, in fact, waste many minutes, hours or even a lifetime hating something or someone.

Most who are trying to live a Christian life, may be taken aback at the suggestion that we hate someone, for scripture clearly states this is not permitted. Yet, many are caught in the trap of hating themselves which greatly diminishes their happiness. They may have physical features they do not like or memories which plague their self-worth. This dislike of self makes it very difficult to love God or others in an open and free way. So, life is lived far beneath its potential, and positive modelling is lost with one's offspring.

To probe even deeper, we dare not "hate things one minute longer" for it drains our strength and creativity. By things I mean our job or career, the place we live, the set of relatives we have, our hereditary looks, the spouse we chose, our "lot in life," or our financial status. The truth is there are many things we cannot change since they are out of our control. Other issues we can alter but probably never will as long as hate dominates our thinking.

It's amazing how fast life goes--a minute here and a moment there and then eternity. Therefore, one minute longer becomes very significant. It's your future and you deserve to have a good one. This writer recommends giving all your hate and heartache to Jesus.

Hebrews 2:3 LB   *What makes us think that we can escape if we are indifferent to this great salvation announced by the Lord Jesus Himself and passed on to us by those who heard Him speak?*

RECUSE YOURSELF

Recuse means to disqualify yourself in a particular setting, to remove yourself from participating to avoid a conflict of interest.

Life is full of situations where we and others would be better off if we recused ourselves. Sometimes we may find ourselves expected to pass judgment on something or someone when we don't know all the facts. This could mean we need to do more fact finding. It also may indicate that things would improve if we simply stepped aside and allowed someone else to deal with the matter.

This is not a cop-out or abdication of duty. Rather, it is a recognition that occasionally issues arise that we are not qualified to decide. For example, as a parent, I may come into the middle of an argument between my child and my spouse. My tendency, as a man, is to defend my wife and overreact which, most likely, compounds the conflict. Staying out of the fray may be the better choice.

Jesus said we're to "let our yes be yes and our no be no." In other words, not only should we be truthful but we're also to avoid settings where we cannot definitively say yes or no, because to do so would likely lead to a misjudgment.

Some people have nothing to say and still insist on saying it. God would have us live at a higher level which models this prayer, "Let the words of my mouth and the meditations of my heart be acceptable in your sight, O Lord, my strength and my Redeemer." Amen!

Matthew 5:33-37   MSG   *And don't say anything you don't mean. This counsel is embedded deep in our traditions. You only make things worse when you lay down a smoke screen of pious talk, saying, 'I'll pray for you,' and never doing it, or saying, 'God be with you,' and not meaning it. You don't make your words true by embellishing them with religious lace. In making your speech sound more religious, it becomes less true. Just say 'yes' and 'no.' When you manipulate words to get your own way, you go wrong.*

SHARIYA MUNGU
(Sharr E Ya Moon Goo)

When my wife and I were missionaries in Kenya we learned a very important Swahili phrase: "Shari Ya Mungu" which means, "It's the problem of God." This saying has helped us many times in all kinds of situations.

Now, all of us have problems. In our better moments we refer to them as challenges and they certainly are that. Bottom line is problems have to be handled in some fashion.

Many things we encounter daily are simply "out of our control." Try as hard as we can, we cannot do anything about the situation or bring effective change. Oh, we often try to modify our circumstances or alter people's perception of us, but still the problem persists, sometimes even flourishes.

When we first heard "Shari Ya Mungu" it seemed rather fatalistic or passive to refer to our problems as God's problems. However, the longer we live the more we realize only God can solve much of the "stuff" we encounter. It is His desire, right from the outset, that we acknowledge our weakness and His strength. Trouble is we tend to consult Him late in the game thereby prolonging our conflict.

Life's lessons are not easy. Repetition seems to be the norm. But, great peace and pleasure comes in surrendering our concerns to the One who can actually do something about them if He chooses. If not, then He'll provide whatever you need to "hang in there." After all, SHARI YA MUNGU!

1 Peter 5:7 LB *Let Him have all your worries and cares, for He is always thinking about you and watching everything that concerns you.*

SMOOTH OR SQUEAKY PRAYERS?

It has been said that "the loudest sound known to man is the rattle in his new car." This bothers us and we usually do not rest until we find the source and eliminate it.

Squeaks seem to have a lower priority. We tend to be more tolerant of them since they only last a second or two. We plan to fix them but often get distracted with "more important matters." Meanwhile the irritating sound reminds us that the moving part is deteriorating right before us. It's amazing that businesses which sell lubricating oils and sprays often neglect their own buildings. Squeaky bathroom doors are almost standard equipment in many stores.

Our prayers can be squeaky, especially if they're infrequent. Little use allows spiritual corrosion which creates friction. We tend to be pushy with God, like the more noise we make the better He'll hear us. Occasional praying can never compensate for consistent praying. Our prayers can come out as desperate and unsure as to whether God can or will answer.

The plan is for us to talk to God continually. The more you talk to someone the easier it is to communicate with that person. God's "chat room" is always open. Our praying will "smooth out" when we sense His nearness. Sometimes we don't have to say a word.

Luke 18:1 LB *One day Jesus told His disciples a story to illustrate their need for constant prayer and to show them that they must keep praying until the answer comes.*

WHAT'S GOOD ABOUT GOOD FRIDAY?

As a kid growing up I was taught the significance of Good Friday. Still, I wondered, "How can death be good?" Jesus died at age thirty-three. What's good about dying so young?

Consider these five good things that happened on Good Friday.

The Right Decision was Made in Gethsemane. Making right decisions is always very important but none so much as when Jesus sweated it out in the garden. He knew of hideous crucifixions. He'd seen others die this way. Like us, Christ had free will. He could have chosen to skip the cross, but he didn't and THAT'S GOOD!

Trumped-Up Charges Only Point to His Innocence and Purity. The Sanhedrin, the supreme court of the Jewish people, tried as hard as they could to eliminate Jesus by breaking all of their own rules during the trial. Our Lord should have been acquitted, but He died for you and me and THAT'S GOOD!

Even Politics Could Not Derail the Plan of Redemption. Christ's case was bounced back and forth from Pilate to Herod. Jurisdiction and political issues could have thwarted the entire crucifixion process which would have left us without a Savior. But, they did not and THAT'S GOOD!

Carrying The Cross of Christ Is Worth It. When Jesus fell to the cobblestones under the heavy weight of the cross, Simon was chosen from the crowd to carry it. His once in a life-time trip to Jerusalem to celebrate Passover was now ruined. But, the story does not end there. Scholars believe that Simon's son, Rufus, is the same one Paul saluted in his Roman letter as a friend and leader. Good Friday tells us to hang in there, that God knows what He's doing. He will more than pay you back for your cross bearing and THAT'S GOOD!

It's Never too Late to Turn to Christ. Dismas, the penitent thief on an adjacent cross, did not know how to properly pray but Jesus always knows how to properly hear. When the Lord said, "Today you'll be with me in paradise," He was saying today you will walk with me in my heavenly garden. You won't just sneak into heaven. You're coming in as a special friend of the King and THAT'S GOOD!

Matthew 27:35-40 MSG *After they had finished nailing Him to the cross and were waiting for Him to die, they whiled away the time by throwing dice for His clothes.*

Above His head they had posted the criminal charge against Him: THIS IS JESUS, THE KING OF THE JEWS. *Along with Him, they also crucified two criminals, one to His right, the other to His left. People passing along the road jeered, shaking their heads in mock lament: "You bragged that you could tear down the Temple and then rebuild it in three days—so show us your stuff! Save yourself! If you're really God's Son, come down from that* cross!"

STOP, LOOK, AND LISTEN

Every New Year as we pass from one date to another, there's always the anticipation of the unknown, the "starting over" and the hope for a better future. No matter what, we all go into a new year with our blessings, challenges and assorted baggage. There are many things in which we have zero control. Our standard of living improves when we focus on things we can control.

Three words most of us learned in kindergarten or first grade are: Stop, Look and Listen. These words have helped us master the art of crossing streets and railroad tracks. They have served us well and are still vital to our survival.

These three words also apply in our relationships. By **Stopping** more and engaging family, friends and even strangers, we'll find our communication improving, and we'll see things we would have missed had we kept going.

Then there's the matter of **Looking;** we fail to "pick up on things" when we're glancing all around and missing the obvious right in front of us. True, it's good to plan ahead but let's not omit today, for it is all we have. Looking can save us many embarrassments and problems.

Listening is never easy but pays so well. To tune into someone else not only enriches them but also embellishes our life. People just want to be heard, and we all can afford to give them that gift.

If we'll practice Stopping, Looking and Listening to others, and more so to our Lord, our future will be "out of this world."

Matthew 7:12 MSG *Here is a simple, rule-of-thumb guide for behavior: Ask yourself what you want people to do for you, then grab the initiative and do it for them.*

SURROUNDED

Old westerns often portray the "bad guys" being sur-rounded by the "good guys." We cheered as right prevailed over wrong. We even knew who was good and who was bad by the color of their hats.

Today we really don't know, for sure, who's causing all the trouble. Evil doers blend in and do their terrorizing and make up the rules as they go. Fighting back is not easy as we try to balance mercy with justice.

Our world is very fearful now. Not knowing what will happen next and to whom, we're tempted to panic and feel defeated with all the senseless carnage. Many innocent people are lying low, altering some of their regular activities, hoping to escape harm and contamination.

There's an Old Testament story which depicts an army encompassing the home of an unpopular prophet. It looks like certain defeat: that death is imminent. But the prophet,

Elisha, sees beyond the obvious to a much larger armed force surrounding his captors.

We too must look further than those without faith, for our Father's angels are circling us. Captain Jesus has never lost a battle!

2 Kings 6:15-17   NIV *When the servant of the man of God got up and went out early the next morning, an army with horses and chariots had surrounded the city. "Oh no, my lord! What shall we do?" the servant asked. "Don't be afraid," the prophet answered. "Those who are with us are more than those who are with them." And Elisha prayed, "Open his eyes, L*ORD*, so that he may see." Then the L*ORD *opened the servant's eyes, and he looked and saw the hills full of horses and chariots of fire all around Elisha.*

TALKING IN LINE

I was standing in line at my bank waiting to be served when, in the line next to me, a young man's phone rang and he answered it. He began a loud conversation with an invisible person which went on for 10 minutes or so, He even continued the talking while being helped by the teller. His use of our "noise space" was rude and thoughtless, to say the least. Other customers endured with me in quiet indignation.

In our world of sophisticated communication, how easy it is to converse with people around the world and ignore those right in front of us. Common courtesy is often sacrificed when we take care of business at the expense of present company.

Most of us encounter the inevitable "wait lines" even in our "online" economy. Whether it be at a grocery checkout, doctor's office, sporting event, movie or wherever, we spend a considerable amount of hours waiting for our name to be called or to hear the word "next."

Since the waiting game cannot be totally avoided, consider making it more productive:

First, try talking to someone in line, not complaining but just being friendly; it will help both of you.

Second, make sure you have a good motivational book in hand in case no one is in the talking mood.

Third, quietly talk to God and ask Him to bless those around you. It will make the wait time go much faster--you can bank on it!

Proverbs 8:34 NLT *Joyful are those who listen to me, watching for me daily at my gates, waiting for me outside my home!*

WHO PRAYS FOR YOU?

Someone once said that prayer is the least developed power source in the world. As energy issues dominate the geopolitical landscape, we do well to give our attention to the subject of prayer for it is real, whether we plug in or not.

Even if you're not a Believer, it is vital that you have someone in your life who knows how to connect with God and can do so on the first ring. You may not practice prayer yourself, but if you're ever in trouble, having someone with a direct line to heaven could make the difference whether you "make it" or not.

In our finite understanding we simply don't know all that's going on around us in the unseen world. God wants us to know more about Him. He desires to interface with us daily. If it's true that knowledge is power and experience says it is, then we must stay open to new information even when it comes from outside our senses.

One of the best things you can do for yourself is to get close to someone who is on a "first-name basis" with God and ask them to regularly pray for you. Don't worry. God will never override your free will, so you can continue to make choices. However, having your name brought before the heavenly throne each day is a win-win situation, both in this world and the one to come.

James 5:16 MSG *Make this your common practice: Confess your sins to each other and pray for each other so that you can live together whole and healed. The prayer of a person living right with God is something powerful to be reckoned with.*

TEACHING AND HEARING

Golf teacher legend Harvey Penick says some interesting things about life. One of his gems states, "It's not what the teacher says, but what the student hears that matters."

Each of us is a teacher to someone: it may be to your kids or maybe someone you supervise at work. Daily we communicate knowledge to someone about some aspect of life. Often we teach and are not even aware of it. The challenge comes when we are aware of our teaching role, and we get discouraged because we feel ineffective. In fact, many times we simply do not connect no matter how you "slice" it.

Harvey is right: the student must be ready to hear and learn. Timing is very pivotal. We go through periods of low receptivity to new instruction. As a teacher we must understand that those we teach, either formally or informally, are not always ready to hear what we say, much less to apply it. Therefore, we need not take it personally as though we have somehow failed. Of course you keep trying and avoid blaming others for your shortcomings. At the same time relax and don't take yourself so seriously.

Jesus, the greatest Teacher to ever live, understood this principle very well. In His parable about the soil types He told us that some good lessons will fall on rocky, thorny and hardened ground. Only a certain percentage would be productive.

The teacher's responsibility is to teach the best they can and leave the results with God. You hear?

Matthew 13:3c-9   LB *A farmer was sowing grain in his fields. As he scattered the seed across the ground, some fell beside a path, and the birds came and ate it. And some fell on rocky soil where there was little depth of earth; the plants sprang up quickly enough in the shallow soil, but the hot sun soon scorched them and they withered and died, for they had so little root. Other seeds fell among thorns, and the thorns choked out the tender blades. But some fell on good soil and produced a crop that was thirty, sixty, and even a hundred times as much as he had planted. If you have ears, listen!"*

YOU CUT ME OFF

I was waiting in the drive-thru line of a fast food restaurant, when out of nowhere, an elderly gentleman tapped on my window and admonished, "Sir, you cut me off!" He tried to explain that I did something wrong in the intersection we had come from, but I never understood my infraction. I immediately apologized and he returned to his car.

One does not have to drive very far or live too long before they find themselves cutting somebody off. It's usually not intentional but a habit we develop when we are hurried, preoccupied or just not paying attention. We cut people off:

VERBALLY. Our tongue is such a useful body part but often gets us into trouble. It certainly is helpful if we think before we speak, even breathing a prayer to say the right words.

EMOTIONALLY. This is a harder category to detect for we never quite know how our conversation will be received.

However, kindness and a gentle voice are proven winners. God will help us with this, but we must let Him.

SPIRITUALLY. It is so easy to judge and secretly label people. We cut them off when we make assumptions about their spirituality with little or no evidence. This can discourage them and hinder our ability to positively influence them.

Too many lives are crashing. Let's not be a contributing cause.

Proverbs 13:3 MSG *Careful words make for a careful life; careless talk may ruin everything.*

THE FACTS DON'T COUNT

Every Easter we are challenged by the implausible events of the Resurrection. When one investigates the idea of Jesus coming back to life after having suffered such an excruciating and inhuman death, it definitely stretches the mind. Yet, we literally base our faith on the belief that Christ actually died and rose again. As someone once remarked, "The facts are interesting but irrelevant."

So often we only know part of the facts. With our partial knowledge we make assumptions as to what is true and what is not. The circumstances which comprise Easter go beyond human understanding for we are dealing with the Divine.

Scripture tells us that His ways are higher than ours. Therefore, a totally different set of facts are operating which we accept by faith while enjoying the resulting benefits. I do not understand electricity, but I can enjoy turning on a light in a dark room or opening a garage door with one touch of a button from my car.

Likewise, I am baffled by the law of aerodynamics, but I can fly from Atlanta to Seattle and still have time for a round of golf.

There are many things in life which make no sense to us but that does not prohibit our use of them. Similarly, the cross, the resurrection, and the empty tomb are beyond our ability to comprehend, but we can enjoy peace and joy in Jesus.

Buying into the gospel message and accepting Christ's gift of salvation is a great way to really enjoy life both now and later.

Hebrews 11:1-2 LB *What is faith? It is the confident assurance that something we want is going to happen. It is the certainty that what we hope for is waiting for us, even though we cannot see it up ahead.*

UNEXCUSED BEHAVIOR

Most of us are appalled as we hear the myriad excuses from our leaders as to why they behave in a certain way. The blame game is threatening the very foundation of our country. It has no healing power but simply fuels mistrust and erodes confidence.

Far too many subscribe to an excuse-ridden lifestyle. It makes them feel better for a while since they convince themselves that "everyone is doing it." Once you start down this path the excuses become more and more ridiculous.

In our relativistic world it's easy to believe that any excuse will work as long as you can blame someone or something for your own choices. Meanwhile, our children watch and size up the situation very quickly, and society continues to deteriorate.

You might be asking, "Well, what can I do about all of this? I'm just an average person trying to get along." True, you may be a regular citizen but you can make a difference. Consider these suggestions:

- Subscribe to objective truth. The Bible makes it very clear that we ARE responsible for our own actions and there ARE consequences for the things we do. Relying on our own sense of right and wrong is like travelling down a road with a bridge out. It's okay for a while but calamity is coming.

- Start today! Monitor your own behavior and do not alibi-out as though someone else made you do it. Be responsible. It's an adult thing.

- Be aware that you are a model to someone. Don't be fooled if those watching you never say anything, for models are designed to watch or study, not to converse.

People we admire the most own up for their actions. It's the only way to truly live!

Psalm 19:14 LB *May my spoken words and unspoken thoughts be pleasing even to you, O Lord my Rock and my Redeemer.*

WATER SHORTAGE

In many parts of the USA, especially the western states, there is a water shortage. Conservation, even rationing of water is in effect. It's been hot and dry for a long time.

There is an old pop song which says, "Shower those you love…" Without the constant watering of kindness and expressions of love the human spirit tends to shrivel up and die. We can literally sap the life and energy of others if we only sprinkle them now and then.

Rain comes down in various forms. From the downpour to a steady drizzle, each drop does its job to reinvigorate Earth thereby producing renewal and growth. Likewise, we all demonstrate love in varied ways, but those closest to us need to be showered; when this happens everybody wins.

We used to sing a song in church titled "Showers of Blessings". It acknowledges God's help but also asks to be inundated with more than mercy, but a "gully washer" of love which cleans out and rids the debris of despair and doubt.

Good news. There is no shortage of water/love with our Lord. He knows just how and when to refresh us. Look up! It looks like rain!

John 4:14 LB *But the water I give them," he said, "becomes a perpetual spring within them, watering them forever with eternal life."*

TOO CLOSE TO CALL

In our 24/7 news world we hear a lot of information, and some of it is conjecture with TV news agencies competing to be the first to cover a story. In political matters such as elections sometimes the race is just "too close to call" even though many professionals are working on it.

Everyday life has things that are too close to call. Sometimes we share information about someone or a situation where we do not have all the facts, yet we somehow feel compelled to speak hoping our analysis or what we have heard is correct. We may think we can get away with this behavior, but it usually is very devastating and costly.

Misjudging others is all too common. We must strive to always give the benefit of the doubt to others. We only see their actions, but God knows their heart. We hear their words, but God knows their motives. Most of the time there are extenuating circumstances under the surface which are unknown to us. What seems to be an attitude or tendency may be totally misleading. Quite often our perception of another person skews our judgment of them; we size them up by how we see them which is not necessarily true.

In our relationships it is good to operate with the "too close to call" guideline which says it is far better to pray for and think the best of others than to make a call on them which can be inaccurate and harmful.

If we ask, God will help us live on this level.

Matthew 7:1 MSG *Don't pick on people, jump on their failures, criticize their faults—unless, of course, you want the same treatment. That critical spirit has a way of boomeranging.*

WHEN YOU DON'T FEEL LIKE PRAYING...

Feelings are an important part of our lives. They add value, are vital to our decision making and differentiate us from the animal world. They make us human, allowing us to experience joy and sadness, sometimes at the same time.

Several years ago a singing group came to my church and their opening number was "When You Don't Feel Like Praying...Pray." So often we really need to pray but just don't feel like doing it. Prayer is work and must be deliberate in order to change us so we can change our situation.

The cooperative relationship God has established with humankind requires continual communication in order to know what He does and what we're supposed to do. Even with instruction from the Bible and respected friends, each of us must still talk to God to clarify and verify His exact will for us.

So, the next time you don't feel like praying, PRAY! It will help you, those around you and allow God to intervene. He's waiting on your call.

Ephesians 6:18a LB *Pray all the time. Ask God for anything in line with the Holy Spirit's wishes.*

YOU DON'T HAVE TO BE ON
STAGE TO BE A STAR

While attending a play with my sister I noticed a statement in the program which arrested my attention: "You don't have to be on stage to be a star." All of us are positioned somewhere on the stage of life. You may be at the front and have many lines to say or you may be in a supportive role with few lines, but they are very vital to the total production.

Each of us is a "star" to someone. You may not feel like a star; in fact, you may sense failure at the very same time you are center stage in someone's life. Plays come and go but life lives on. To someone, maybe a spouse, a child or a neighbor, YOU ARE A STAR, a hero. They admire you in ways they cannot express.

Sometimes, in God's providence, you may learn of the positive impact you're having on someone. When or if that happens thank God and keep on rehearsing, for most of life is a rehearsal.

In a play, often the lead characters are not what makes the play great. It is the support cast which carries the story and makes it work. Likewise, most of us are in support roles and that's okay. Shakespeare said, "All the World's a Stage."

So, play your part well, enjoy the journey and don't forget, to someone you are THE STAR!

Ephesians 5:2 LB Be *full of love for others, following the example of Christ who loved you and gave himself to God as a sacrifice to take away your sins. And God was pleased, for Christ's love for you was like sweet perfume to Him.*

TOO BIG FOR ME

Life is a wonderful gift but can be challenging and difficult at times. Most of us have been programmed to be self-sufficient, to handle our own problems the best we can and this is good. But, days come and situations arise that are too big for us. What do we do then?

Ignoring our problems may be a quick fix but does not work; We can only tread water so long. Avoiding reality may be a temporary placebo, but life will catch us eventually. It's only a matter of time.

So, what do you do when the roaring waves threaten to drown you? Here are some things I'm learning:

- Admit you need help, that you cannot handle it alone. When you do this your hope factor will begin to rise.

- Understand it may be too big for you but never too big for God. Performing miracles for His children is one of His favorite activities. But, we have to ask and trust.

- Stay open to help from all kinds of sources. Incremental answers tend to be God's way of allowing us to remain a part of the solution.

- Stop looking at your watch, you're on His time. Resignation to "whenever" releases peace and strength to finish the race.

Ps 121:1-2   MSG *I look up to the mountains; does my strength come from mountains? No, your strength comes from GOD, Who made heaven, and earth, and mountains.*

WHY IS THE BOOK NAMED CODE BILLY?

This second volume of CODE BILLY is a group of meditations written and compiled as inspired by my daughter's struggle to survive and overcome a devastating stroke at age 26. When Saralyn was released from rehab hospital she received a "Code Billy" farewell. (named after a patient who spent many months in the hospital) All her doctors, nurses and other hospital personnel lined the hallway to applaud her recovery and wish her a wonderful life.

ABOUT THE AUTHOR

- Married to Marg Dorsey for 42 years with four adult children

- Graduate of Ohio Christian University and George Fox Seminary

- Travelled, sang and played gospel music for eight years

- Pastored nine churches in Oregon; Alberta, Canada; Indiana; Georgia; Ohio; and Nairobi, Kenya

- Teaches personality and leadership seminars

- **Author of *CODE BILLY-75 Real Life Meditations***